COUNTRYWISE

FRANCE
AND FRENCH

Nicola Wright

Chrysalis Children's Books

Contents

This edition published in 2003 by
Chrysalis Children's Books
64 Brewery Road, London N7 9NT

Copyright © Chrysalis Books PLC

Edited by Dee Turner
Designed by Teresa Foster
Additional illustration by Guy Smith
Cover design by Keren-Orr Greenfeld
Consultant Claire Nozières
Typeset by Diane Pullen

A CIP catalogue record for this book is available
from the British Library

ISBN 184138 475 5

Printed in China
10 9 8 7 6 5 4 3 2 1

About this book

In this book you can find out about France – its people, landscapes and language. For example, discover what the French like to eat and drink, what they do for a living, and what famous French places look like.

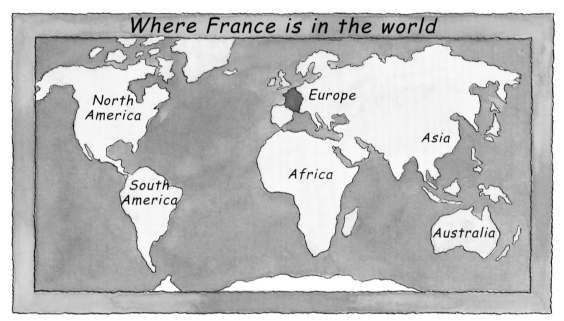

Where France is in the world

North America

Europe

Asia

Africa

South America

Australia

Find out, also, what school-days are like for French children, and about their holidays and festivals. On page 26 there is a special section to introduce you to speaking French.

Hello!

Bonjour!

It explains how to use and pronounce everyday words and phrases, so you can make friends and ask for things in cafés and shops. Also, some French words and their meaning are given throughout the book to help you increase your vocabulary.

Map of France

France is one of the largest countries in Europe. It is bordered by eight other countries: Spain, Andorra, Monaco, Switzerland, Luxembourg, Germany, Belgium and Italy. Even so, almost half of France's border is coastline.

Longest river:
The Loire, 1,020 km. Many beautiful châteaux line its banks.

le fleuve
river

Corsica

France owns the island of Corsica. It lies in the Mediterranean Sea, 170 km south of France.

The French landscape varies greatly. In some places there are high mountains and thick forests. In others there are rolling fields and sandy beaches.

la carte
map

Dieppe

English Channel

Cherbourg

Le Havre

Rouer

Caen

Normandy

Brest

St Malo

Brittany

Rennes

Le Mans

Loire Valley

Loire

Nantes

Centre

Poitou-Charent

Limog

Limousir

Bordeaux

Dordogne

Garonne

Aquitaine

Midi-Pyrénées

Pyrenees

Spain

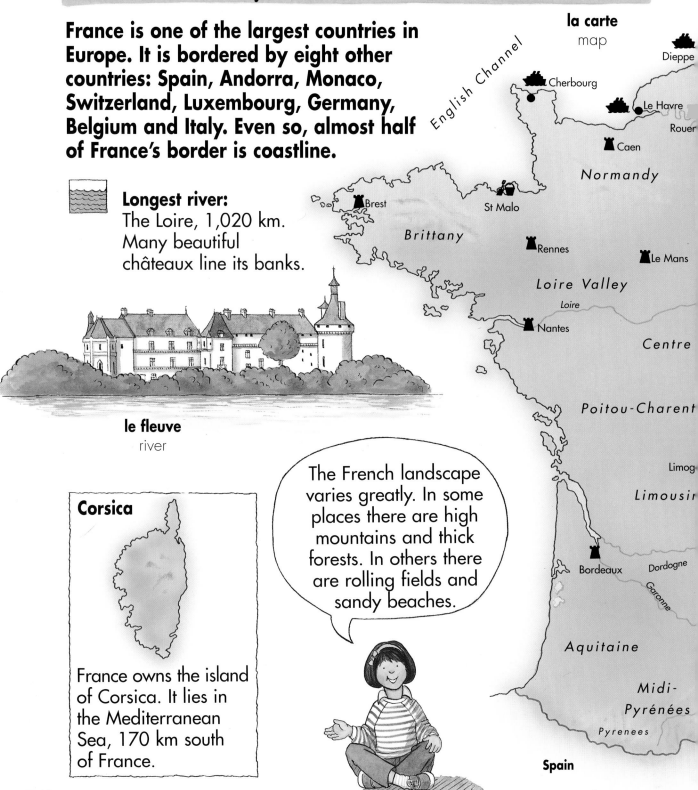

4

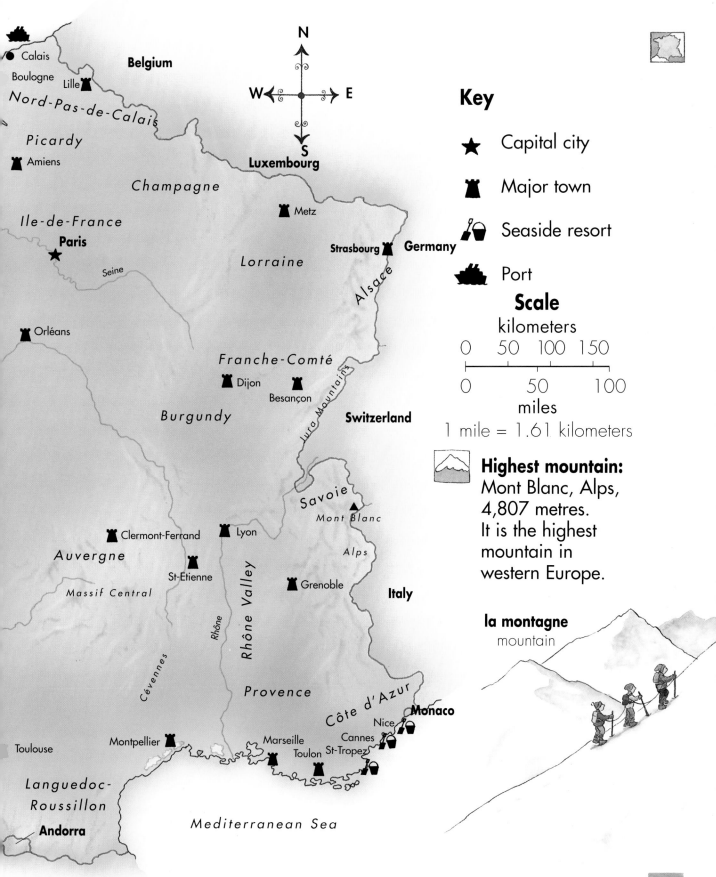

Calais
Boulogne
Lille
Belgium
Nord-Pas-de-Calais

N
W ← → E
S

Key

★ Capital city

♟ Major town

🪣 Seaside resort

🚢 Port

Picardy
Amiens

Champagne

Luxembourg

Metz

Ile-de-France
Paris

Lorraine

Strasbourg **Germany**

Alsace

Seine

Orléans

Franche-Comté
Dijon
Besançon
Jura Mountains

Switzerland

Burgundy

Savoie
Mont Blanc

Clermont-Ferrand

Auvergne
St-Etienne

Lyon

Alps

Grenoble

Italy

Massif Central

Cévennes

Rhône

Rhône Valley

Provence

Côte d'Azur

Monaco
Nice
Cannes
St-Tropez

Toulouse

Montpellier

Marseille
Toulon

Languedoc-Roussillon

Andorra

Mediterranean Sea

Scale
kilometers
0   50   100   150

0   50   100
miles
1 mile = 1.61 kilometers

Highest mountain:
Mont Blanc, Alps,
4,807 metres.
It is the highest
mountain in
western Europe.

la montagne
mountain

5

Facts about France

Although France is twice as large as the United Kingdom, about the same number of people live there, so it is much less crowded.

Size:
543,965 sq km

Population:
56,647,000

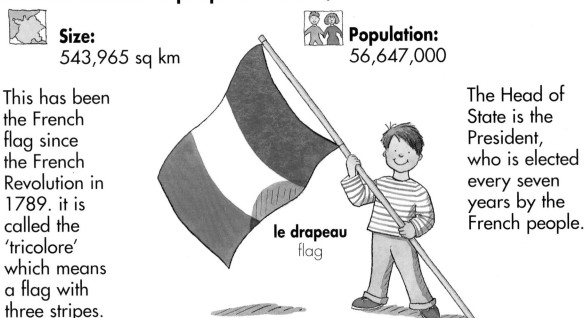

This has been the French flag since the French Revolution in 1789. it is called the 'tricolore' which means a flag with three stripes.

le drapeau
flag

The Head of State is the President, who is elected every seven years by the French people.

Language

Breton is spoken in the north-west. It is related to Cornish, Welsh and Irish.

Although the official language is French, there are other languages spoken in parts of the country:

la langue
language

Basque is spoken in the region around the Spanish border. It is unlike any other European language.

A dialect of German is spoken in Alsace and Lorraine. These areas used to belong to Germany.

Money

The currency used in France is the euro.

France is not the only country to use euros. On January 1 2002, twelve countries in Europe began to use euro notes and coins. All euros can be used in any of those twelve countries.

le billet de banque
banknote

One euro can be split into 100 cents. Coins are made in amounts of 1 and 2 euros and 1, 2, 5, 10, 20 and 50 cents. Notes are made in amounts of 5, 20, 50, 100, 200, and 500 euros.

la piece de monnaie
coin

Capital city:
Paris

Some things France is well-known for

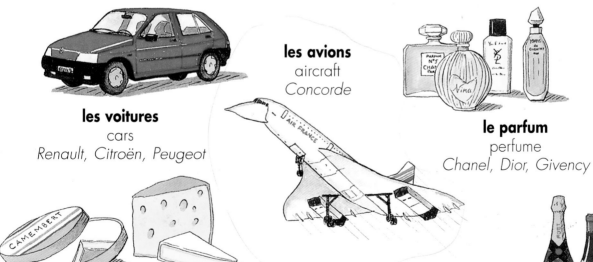

les avions
aircraft
Concorde

les voitures
cars
Renault, Citroën, Peugeot

le parfum
perfume
Chanel, Dior, Givency

le fromage
cheese
Camembert, Brie and about 400 other varieties

le vin
wine
Champagne, Burgundy, Bordeaux and many others

7

Regions of France

France is divided into many different regions, and includes the island of Corsica in the Mediterranean. The scenery, weather and way of life vary greatly from region to region.

The north of France has cold winters, warm summers, and plenty of rainfall.

le temps
weather

le nord
north

le sud
south

In the south of France it is hot and dry in the summer and mild and moist in the winter.

Many of the seaside resorts along the south coast, such as Cannes and Nice, were once small fishing ports. Now they are holiday places for rich, fashionable people from all over Europe.

The French call the south coast the 'Côte d'Azur', which means 'sky-blue coast', because of its good weather.

le ski nautique
waterskiing

About one-fifth of France is covered with woodland. In the Vosges and Jura mountains in the east there are large pine and fir forests.

la forêt
forest

Wild animals, including boar, foxes, beavers and chamois (a kind of antelope) can be found in these regions.

8

In the east, the high mountains of the Alps are covered with snow all year and the scenery is spectacular.

le ski
skiing

This region is very popular for skiing in the winter and hiking in summer.

la neige
snow

Normandy, in the north, has a flat coastline with long sandy beaches.

la côte
coast

The coastline of Brittany in the north-west is rocky with many inlets.

la plage
beach

Several large rivers run through the high, flat land of central France. Beautiful countryside and picturesque towns line their banks.

There are vineyards all over France. Most regions produce their own wine. Champagne and Burgundy are some of the best known.

le raisin
grapes

le vignoble
vineyard

9

Paris

Paris is the largest and most important French city. It is the capital of the country and the centre of industry, business, fashion and entertainment.

The original city was built on an island in the middle of the River Seine. The island became known as the Ile de la Cité (City Island). During the 12th century, the beautiful Notre-Dame cathedral was built on it.

Notre-Dame Cathedral

l'artiste
artist

Paris is famous for its arts. There are many street painters in the district called Montmartre. Famous artists like Renoir and Picasso once lived there.

The quickest and cheapest way to get around the city is on the Métro underground railway.

Over 9,000,000 people live in Paris and its suburbs, which is almost one-fifth of the total French population.

les gens
peoples

Famous places

Palais de Louvre and the glass pyramids (art gallery)

Sacré-Cœur
(a church on top of the hill of Montmartre with splendid views of Paris)

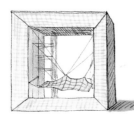

Arche de la Défense
(built to mark 200 years since the French Revolution)

Arc de Triomphe
(the Tomb of the Unknown Soldier is under it)

Eiffel Towel
(built in 1889 for an exhibition)

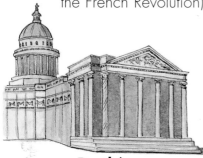

Panthéon
(church containing the tombs of some of those people who died during the Revolution)

Place de la Concorde
(many people were guillotined here during the Revolution)

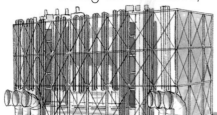

Pompidou Centre
(modern exhibition halls)

Moulin Rouge
(one of the most famous nightclubs in Paris)

In a typical French town

There is a square in the middle of most French towns and villages. All the main shops are grouped around it. Often there is a statue or water fountain in the centre.

la boulangerie
baker's

le magasin
shop

le tabac
tobacconist

People gather to talk in the main square under the shade of trees.

la charcuterie
pork butcher's

le supermarché
supermarket

Les agents de police work in the towns.
Les gendarmes work in the country.
Both types of police wear a blue uniform.

la poste
post office

l'épicerie-alimentation
grocer's

la librairie-papeterie-mason de la presse
bookshop-stationers-newspaper shop

12

l'hôtel de ville
town hall

l'église
church

There are lots of churches in France. Most people are Roman Catholic.

la banque
bank

la pharmacie
chemist's

la droguerie
hardware store

la patisserie-confiserie
cake and sweet shop

le boucherie
butcher's

Boules (bowls) is a popular traditional game. A small metal ball is thrown on the ground. Each person throws a larger metal ball so that it lands as near to the little one as possible. Points are scored for landing nearest to the small ball.

la boutique de vêtements
clothes shop

le syndicat d'initiative
tourist information

13

Eating in France

The French are famous for their love of food and cooking. Meals are never rushed and French restaurants are some of the best in the world.

Here is a typical French breakfast (le petit déjeuner) called a continental breakfast:

la confiture
jam

le beurre
butter

We drink our coffee or chocolate from bowls, and we like to dip bread into it.

la baguette
long French loaf

le café
coffee

le croissant
flaky, crescent-shaped roll

le chocolat chaud
hot chocolate

Here are some typical French dishes.

le bœuf bourguignon
a beef stew cooked in red wine

la salade niçoise

la quiche lorraine
bacon and egg flan

olives, anchovies, tomatoes, onion and tuna fish

les crêpes
pancakes

les escargots
snails

la tarte aux pommes
apple flan

les moules
mussels

le pâté
pâté

l'apéritif
aperitif
Pernod, Ricard

Some well-known French drinks.

le vin
wine
Champagne, Burgundy, Muscadet

la bière
beer
usually made in Alsace

le cidre
cider

made in Normandy and Brittany

la liqueur
liqueur
Kirsch, Chartreuse

l'eau minérale
mineral water
Evian (still), Perrier (fizzy)

A French meal

Lunch (le déjeuner) and dinner (le diner) are usually large meals and can go on for hours.

le repas
meal

The meal starts with soup or crudités (raw salad or vegetables). Next there is a meat or fish course. The vegetables are often eaten after this.

The meal ends with cheese, followed by a pudding or fruit.

What people do

France is a large country, and people live and work differently in the various regions. Some people work in busy industrial areas. Others live in the countryside and are farmers.

France is an important farming country, but today machines do much of the work. Fewer people now work on the land than in industry.

Farmers grow cereals (wheat, oats and barley), grapes, fruit and vegetables. Dairy farmers produce cheese, butter, milk, cream and yoghurt.

le fermier
farmer

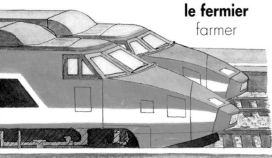

French railways employ many people. France's Train à Grande Vitesse (TGV) runs between towns all over the country and holds the world rail speed record.

Sheep farming is common in the south-east and the central plateau. Roquefort cheese is made from sheep's milk.

France is especially famous for its wine. The wine business employs many people, especially in the grape-picking season. The wines and brandies of France are sold all over the world.

le mouton
sheep

Steel, cars, shipbuilding, aircraft, textiles, perfume and food products are some of France's main industries.

l'usine
factory

French farms and fisheries produce almost all the food the people need.

The people of Brittany (called Bretons) are mainly farmers and fishermen. Nearly a half of the fish caught in the sea around France come from this region.

le pêcheur
fisherman

Figs, oranges, lemons, almonds and olives are grown in the south, along the Mediterranean coast. Flowers are grown there, too, for making perfume. The perfume business is very important.

Many French people work in hotels and restaurants. There is an important tourist trade, especially in the Alps and along the Mediterranean coast.

Brasserie

Le Bistro

17

Children in France

Here you can find out something about school life in France, and about how French children spend their time.

l'école
school

The school day usually begins at 8.30 in the morning and lasts until 4.00 in the afternoon. There may be classes on Saturday mornings, but Wednesdays are normally free.

les vacances
holidays

School children have quite long holidays. They get: one week at Toussaint (All Saints) which is the autumn half-term; two weeks at Christmas; two weeks at the end of February (winter half-term); two weeks at Easter, and two months in the summer.

les devoirs
homework

At most French schools, children do not wear a uniform. Many of them wear jeans, a sweatshirt and trainers.

les vêtements
clothes

Though French children have long holidays, many of them have to do 'devoirs de vacances' (holiday homework), revising what they have learned at school during the year.

18

Many schools also offer what they call 'classe de neige' (class in the snow) or 'classe de mer' (class by the sea). The whole class spends a week in a ski resort or at the seaside. Lessons go on as usual, but the children also do outdoor activities.

All children take part in sports at school.

le sport
sport

Athletics, gymnastics and team sports such as football, volley ball and basketball are played.

le skateboard
skateboarding

As in many other countries, there are crazes. Over recent years these have included skateboarding and electronic games.

One of the favourite pastimes of many French children is reading comics. Characters such as Asterix and Tintin are very popular.

la bande dessinée
comic

History of France

58 B.C.

The Romans, led by Julius Caesar, invaded France (or Gaul, as it was then called). It remained part of the huge Roman Empire for 400 years.

1066

le roi
king

William the Conqueror (from Normandy, in northern France), invaded England, won the Battle of Hastings, and was crowned king of England.

1337–1453

During the Hundred Years War, England invaded France. The English won parts of France, but Joan of Arc inspired the French to rise up against them. She was captured by the English and burned to death in 1431. By 1453 the English had been defeated.

1789

In 1789 the French people decided to overthrow the king and nobles so the people themselves could rule the country. King Louis XVI, and many others, were beheaded. This was called the French Revolution.

le soldat
soldier

1804

'Liberty leading the people'
– a painting by Delacroix

1830–1848

Napoleon Bonaparte was a brilliant soldier, who became the people's hero during the French Revolution. He crowned himself Emperor in 1804. He was defeated by the English at the Battle of Waterloo in 1815.

After the Battle of Waterloo, the French royal family and nobles tried to return to power. However, they were defeated by the people in two more revolutions in 1830 and 1848.

1919

During World War II (1939–1945), Hitler's troops invaded France. General Charles de Gaulle led the French Resistance fighters who worked to defeat the Germans. France was eventually freed in 1944.

1944

France lost the regions of Alsace and Lorraine to Germany during the Franco-Prussian War in 1870. However, at the Treaty of Versailles at the end of World War I (1914–1918), Germany gave them back to France.

1958

In 1958 France joined with West Germany, Italy, Belgium, the Netherlands and Luxembourg to form the European Economic Community.

Famous places

Thousands of tourists from all over the world visit France every year. There are many beautiful and interesting places to see. Here are some of them.

Near Paris is the enormous and magnificent royal palace called the Château de Versailles, built 300 years ago for King Louis XIV.

le pique-nique
picnic

Visitors picnic beside the many lakes, fountains and statues in the grounds.

Mont-Saint-Michel was built as a monastery on a tiny island off the coast of Normandy. When the tide is low, you can walk or drive to it across the sand.

l'île
island

le lac
lake

Annecy is a beautiful old lake-side town in the Savoie region. Visitors like to go boating on the lake.

le pont
bridge

The Pont du Gard is a huge aqueduct in Provence, built over 2,000 years ago by the Romans. It carried spring water 35 km into the town of Nîmes.

The old town of Rouen in Normandy has an important place in French history. It was here that Joan of Arc was burned to death by the English for leading the French against them. A monument marks where she was burned.

Jeanne d'Arc
Joan of Arc

The Château de Chambord, in the Loire Valley, is one of France's most extravagant châteaux. It has 440 rooms and a maze of staircases and turrets.

Corsica, a lovely island in the Mediterranean Sea, is a popular place for holidays. You can enjoy deep-sea diving in the clear, warm water.

la plage
beach

Festivals

The French love celebrations. Many festivals are held throughout the year. Some celebrate religious occasions and historical events, others the arts. Some regions have their own festivals.

On 14 July, everyone in France celebrates the storming of the Bastille prison at the beginning of the French Revolution. There are torchlit processions, military parades and firework displays. People decorate their houses with flags and dance in the streets all night.

la fête
festival

le festival du film
film festival

There are many festivals celebrating the arts, including theatre, cinema, dance and music. The International Film Festival, held in Cannes every year, attracts famous stars and film-makers who come to see the year's new films.

In some parts of northern France, huge models of local historical heroes (called Les Géants (the giants) are paraded through the streets during special festivals.

At Christmas, people ski down the mountains at night carrying flaming torches.

le géant
giant

In the big wine-producing areas, local people celebrate the end of the grape harvest every autumn.

They hold dances and taste the new wine. Members of the wine societies dress up in traditional costumes.

le cyclisme
cycling

The Tour de France is a cycle race that is held each summer. Cyclists from all over the world take part. Millions watch the race, either along the route or on television.

l'âne
donkey

On 6 December, people in the north and east celebrate the Festival of St Nicolas (Father Christmas), the patron saint of children. In many towns a man dressed as St Nicolas walks through the streets with a donkey, handing out sweets to children.

On 6 January the French celebrate la Fête des Rois (festival of the three kings). People eat a special cake, and whoever finds the bean hidden in it is King or Queen of the Day.

A huge carnival is held in Nice to celebrate Mardi Gras (Shrove Tuesday). For 12 days people watch the processions of colourful floats and people in fancy dress.

You can join in a battle of flowers with the people on floats.

le char
float

le cortège
procession

Speaking French

You will find some useful, everyday French words on the following pages, plus some simple phrases that you can use to ask for things.

You will see that every word is written in three different ways:

une orange pressée —— these are the French words

(ewn oronj pressay)

an orange juice

this gives you an idea of how to pronounce the French

this is what it means in English

In each speech bubble you will find a French phrase, a guide to pronouncing it and its English meaning. You will see how easy it is to go shopping or to order what you want to eat and drink at a café.

le kiosque
kiosk

Je voudrais une glace —— the French words

(Jer voodray ewn glass)

I would like an ice-cream

how to pronounce the French words

the English translation

Making friends

Here are some easy French phrases to use when you want to make friends. Down the side of the page are other useful words and phrases that will be helpful in all kinds of situations.

Oui
(*Wee*)
Yes

S'il vous plaît
(*See-voo-play*)
Please

Bonjour
(*Bon-joor*)
Hello

Pardon
(*Par-don*)
Sorry

Monsieur
(*Moosyer*)
Mr

Mademoiselle
(*Madmwazell*)
Miss

**Bonjour.
Comment t'appelles-tu?**
(*Bon-joor. Common tappell-tew?*)
Hello. What is your name?

**Je m'appelle
Mary. Et toi?**
(*Jer mappell Marree. Ay twa?*)
My name is Mary.
And yours?

**Où passes-tu
les vacances?**
(*Oo pass-tew lay vackonss?*)
Where are you staying
on holiday?

J'habite là-bas.
(*Jabeet lah-bah.*)
I live over there.

Quel âge as-tu?
(*Kell arj ah-tew?*)
How old are you?

J'ai douze ans.
(*Jay dooze ong.*)
I'm twelve.

Non
(*Non*)
No

Merci
(*Mairsee*)
Thank you

Au revoir
(*Orvwar*)
Goodbye

Excusez-moi
(*Exkewzay-mwah*)
Excuse me

Madame
(*Madam*)
Mrs

Parlez-vous anglais?
(*Parlay-voo onglay?*)
Do you speak English?

At the café

un sandwich au fromage
(*urn sandweech oh fromarj*)
a cheese sandwich

le sel et le poivre
(*ler sell ay ler pwarvr*)
salt and pepper

une glace à la fraise
(*ewn glass ala frayze*)
a strawberry ice-cream

Monsieur
(*moosyer*)
waiter

la carte
(*lah cart*)
menu

un verre
(*urn vair*)
a glass

un croque-monsieur
(*urn crock moosyer*)
toasted cheese and
ham sandwich

Here you can see people ordering at a café using the phrase Je voudrais, which means I would like. Using this simple phrase you can order any of the items around the picture.

Qu'est-ce que je vous sers, Messieurs?
(*Kessker jer voo sair, Messyer?*)
What can I get you?

Je voudrais un sandwich au fromage et un Coca.
(*Jer voodray urn sondweech oh fromarj ay urn Coca.*)
I would like a cheese sandwich and a Coca-Cola.

une orange pressée
(*ewn oronj pressay*)
an orange juice

des frites
(*day freet*)
some chips

un sandwich au jambon)
(*urn sandweech oh jombon*)
a ham sandwich

une salade mixte
(*ewn salad meext*)
a mixed salad

une glace au chocolate
(*ewn glass oh shokolah*)
a chocolate ice-cream

Je voudrais une glace.
(*Jer voodray ewn glass.*)
I would like an ice-cream.

Madame
(*madam*)
waitress

Quel parfum – fraise, chocolate ou vanille?
(*Kell parfoom – frayze, shokolah ooh vanill?*)
Which flavour – strawberry, chocolate or vanilla?

l'addition
(*lad-ee-see-on*)
the bill

Monsieur! L'addition, s'il vous plait.
(*Moosyer! Lad-ee-see-onh see-voo-play.*)
Waiter! The bill, please.

un Coca
(*urn Coca*)
a Coca-Cola

une glace à la vanille
(*ewn glass ala vanill*)
a vanilla ice-cream

une carafe d'eau
(*ewn caraf doe*)
a jug of water

une petit pain au chocolat
(*urn petee pan oh shokolah*)
a chocolate-filled pastry roll

29

At the shops

les pommes de terre
(*lay pomm der tair*)
potatoes

les framboises
(*lay frombwarz*)
raspberries

les saucisses
(*lay sohseess*)
sausages

le lait
(*ler lay*)
milk

The children are shopping for fruit (les fruits) and vegetables (les légumes) in a grocery shop (épicerie-alimentation).

le pain
(*ler pan*)
bread

Puis-je vous aider?
(*Pwee-jer voos-ayday?*)
Can I help you?

Oui s'il vous plaît. Je voudrais un kilo de pommes.
(*Wee see-voo-play. Jer voodray urn keelo der pomm.*)
Yes please. I would like one kilo of apples.

les timbres
(*lay tambr*)
stamps

la confiture
(*lah konfeetyoor*)
jam

les bonbons
(*lay bon-bon*)
sweets

les poissons
(*lay pwahsson*)
fish

30

le chou-fleur
(*ler shoo-flurr*)
cauliflower

le poulet
(*ler poolay*)
chicken

la bande dessinée
(*lah band desseenay*)
comic

Around the picture are some useful words for things you might want to buy in other shops using the same phrase Je voudrais.

les poires
(*lay pwar*)
pears

Combien en voudriez-vous?
(*Combeeyen on voo-dree-ay-voo?*)
How many would you like?

Deux laitues, s'il vous plaît.
(*Durr laytwo, see-voo-play.*)
Two lettuces, please.

les œufs
(*lez urf*)
eggs

le gâteau
(*ler gattoh*)
cake

le journal
(*ler joor-nal*)
newspaper

les biscuits
(*lay bee-skwee*)
biscuits

le jouet
(*ler jeway*)
toy

un
(*urn*)

deux
(*durr*)

trois
(*trwa*)

quatre
(*kattr*)

cinq
(*sank*)

six
(*seess*)

sept
(*set*)

huit
(*weet*)

neuf
(*nerf*)

dix
(*deess*)

janvier
(*jonveeyay*)
January

noir
(*nwar*)
black

blanc
(*blon*)
white

rouge
(*rooj*)
red

jaune
(*joan*)
yellow

vert
(*vair*)
green

bleu
(*bler*)
blue

lundi
(*lurndee*)
Monday

mardi
(*mardee*)
Tuesday

février
(*fevreeyay*)
February

mars
(*marss*)
March

avril
(*avreel*)
April

mai
(*may*)
May

juin
(*jwan*)
June

juillet
(*jweeyay*)
July

août
(*oot*)
August

septembre
(*septombr*)
September

mercredi
(*mairkrerdee*)
Wednesday

jeudi
(*jerdee*)
Thursday

vendredi
(*vondrerdee*)
Friday

samedi
(*samdee*)
Saturday

dimanche
(*deemonsh*)
Sunday

décembre
(*dayssombr*)
December

novembre
(*novombr*)
November

octobre
(*ocktobr*)
October

32